Text copyright © 2000-
Rose & Michelle Rose
Jesus in the Passover
All rights reserved. This book or any portion thereof may not be reproduced or used in any manner whatsoever
without the express written permission of the publisher except for the use of brief quotations and in a book review.

Printed in the United States of America
First, 2014

ISBN-13: 978-1497407916

ISBN-10:1497407915

Library of Congress Catalogue-in-Publication Data Available
Library of Congress Control Number On File

The Entertainment Industry Chaplains
PO BOX 22231
Saint Paul MN 55122

SPECIAL THANK YOU TO:
Kim Marsh @ Good News Feet
For the use of her artwork

CONTENT

JESUS IS IN THE PASSOVER STORY! 4
- Foreward 4
- Introduction 6
- The Passover Seder 18
  - Ceremonial Garments 19
  - Lighting of the Candles 20
  - The Traditional Washing of the hands 21
  - Explanation of the Four Cups 24
- THE FIRST CUP 29
  - The Blessing 29
  - The Child asks a Question: 30
- The Maggid 31
  - The Child asks the First Question: 42
  - The Child asks the Second Question: 44
- The Seder Plate 45
  - The Seder Plate Items 48
  - The Child asks the Third Question: 48
  - The Child asks the Fourth Question: 56
  - Why is this significant? 58
- The Second Cup 60
- The Meal 65
- After the Meal: 65
  - The Search for the Afikomen 66
- The Third Cup 70
- Cup of Elijah 72
- The Fourth Cup 77

AUTHOR'S BIOGRAPHIES 80
- Tov Rose 80
- Michelle Rose 83
- Mike Rose 84

Jesus is in the Passover Story!

Foreward

By Mike Rose

As a young boy, I can remember the fond memories of Passover. It was a special time for me. My two sisters and I were living with my grandparents in Queens, New York, since my mother had passed away at a very early age. Every year, just before Passover, my grandmother would take out the Passover china and the special sterling silverware. The china and silverware was never used at any other time of the year. My sisters and I would help polish the silverware and silver candle sticks for the occasion, but the most exciting part of the Passover celebration, was our annual trip to the Bronx. I couldn't wait for this time of year because my great-aunt Sophie made the best tasting and fluffiest kneidlach (matzo balls) in the world. I remember sitting in the back seat of my grandfather's car, observing how he gently moved the steering wheel slightly to the right, and then to the left, in order to keep the car in his lane of the parkway. The anxiety was unbearable, until I saw the familiar brownstones, as we approached Marcy Place and the apartment building where my grandmother and grandfather had once lived, prior to moving out to queens. The family had a ninety-nine year lease on that rent-subsidized apartment, so when my grandparents moved to Queens, my aunt and uncle moved into it. Just being in that apartment reminded me of the many enjoyable times I had there, when my grandparents had lived there. I was born only a few blocks away, and I would, many years later, discover that my lovely wife of forty-three years, live only two blocks from there also.

The Passovers I grew up with were very different from what you are about to read here.

Introduction

Jesus the Messiah in the Passover Story

If Passover is a celebration of the miracles God performed in Egypt to free the Israeli's, then why should Christians celebrate this feast? If we accept the Bible as the inerrant Word of God, then we must look at Deuteronomy 16:16-17 (JPS-1917) for the answer:

> "Three times in a year shall all thy males appear before the LORD thy God in the place which He shall choose; on the feast of unleavened bread, and on the feast of weeks, and on the feast of tabernacles; and they shall not appear before the LORD empty; every man shall give as he is able, according to the blessing of the LORD thy God which He hath given thee." (KJV)

Notice also the context of 1 Corinthians 5:5-8 as Paul is talking to non-Jewish Christians:

> "[6]Your glorying *is* not good. Know ye not that a little leaven leaveneth the whole lump? [7]Purge out therefore the old leaven, that ye may be a new lump, as ye are unleavened. For even Messiah our Passover is sacrificed for us: [8]Therefore let us keep the feast, not with old leaven, neither with the leaven of malice and wickedness; but with the unleavened *bread* of sincerity and truth. (KJV)

Why should non-Jewish Christians celebrate Passover? Because it teaches all about Jesus! Passover is an important event to Christians. Until approximately 320 A.D., all Jewish and non-Jewish followers of Yeshua[1] (Jesus) followed the tradition and ceremony of Passover, because it is commemorates the inaugural ceremony of the creation of the New Covenant between God and man!

The feast of Passover precedes the Feast of Unleavened Bread by one day. Today, worldwide, Jews celebrate Passover as an eight day holiday, but Leviticus 23 clearly says it is a one day Feast, followed by the seven day Feast of Unleavened Bread. Shortly, I will show you how it is the first of four feasts of the Lord celebrated at this time of year.

Perhaps you're still wondering what Jesus has to do with Passover?

Well, Jesus is Jewish. He celebrated Passover every year while He dwelt among us on the earth, and He is clearly pictured in every the symbol of Passover. If you want to understand Jesus and His ministry better, it's a great idea to understand Passover!

The story of Passover is the story of Israeli liberation from bondage. It is also the story our liberation from bondage to sin. It is the promise of redemption.

As one goes through the story of Passover, you see the life and mission of the Lamb of God, who takes away the sin of the world. You will see His death, His resurrection, and the promise of His return within the elements and practices of the Passover Seder.

Now let us read Luke 22:7-13:

---

[1] In this teaching the names Yeshua and Jesus are used interchangeably.

> *"Then came the day of Unleavened Bread on which the Passover lamb had to be sacrificed. Jesus sent Peter and John, saying, "Go and make preparations for us to eat the Passover." "Where do you want us to prepare for it?" they asked. He replied, "As you enter the city, a man carrying a jar of water will meet you. Follow him to the house that he enters, and say to the owner of the house, 'The Teacher asks: Where is the guest room, where I may eat the Passover with my disciples?' He will show you a large upper room, all furnished. Make preparations there. They left and found things just as Jesus had told them. So they prepared the Passover." (NIV)*

Passover today is actually three holidays rolled into one. In reality, these three special days are in order:

1) **The Feast of Passover**—the day the Lambs were sacrifices
2) **The Feast of Unleavened Bread**—the celebration of "sinless" bread lasting seven days
3) **The Feast of First Fruits**—the celebration of the first harvest after winter, the Barley Harvest. Specifically, the day the sheaves of Barley were waved before the God.

Jesus was asking Peter and John to go to prepare "for us to eat." Meaning that there are some specific things that have to be put in order for this meal to take place on Passover. In Hebrew, we call this order a "Seder." This Seder is designed to help people understand the imagery and prophesy embedded in the Passover, The Feast of Unleavened Bread and The Feast of First Fruits.

Notice in the passage above, there was a man carrying a jar of water? What is so important about that? Why do all three synoptic gospels tell us about this man? The jar of water is very significant, but the significance is often overlooked because of lack of knowledge. The man carrying the jar of water was returning from the **Pool of Siloam (aka Siloah, or Solomon's pool)** with "Holy Water." This is also the place from which water was drawn for use in Temple sacrificial rituals and purification ceremonies. The Pool of Siloam is where the priest drew their Holy Water using silver pitchers to offer drink offerings to God.

Why is this significant? The pouring out of water in the Old Testament was symbolic of the pouring out of the Holy Spirit. The Holy Spirit was represented in the Old Testament and in Temple rituals long before the Holy Spirit was given for all believers on the Feast of Shavuot (Pentecost) seven weeks after the resurrection of Jesus.

This man carrying a pitcher of water was taking this "Holy Water" from the Pool of Siloam to his own home to be used to wash the hands of those gathered for the Passover! They were to be symbolically washed in the Holy Spirit!

Passover, *the fourteenth day of Nisan in the modern Jewish calendar* (Leviticus: 23:5), is the feast that commemorates the miracles that surrounded His bringing the Children of Israel[2] out of bondage in Egypt.

The miracles performed by God through Moses and Aaron are examples to us of God's provision in the midst of struggle. The judgments of God are repeated in the Book of

---

[2] *In scripture, the term "Children of Israel" refers to the Abrahamic Covenant and to the descendants of Jacob, whose name was changed by God to Israel. (Gen 32:28)*

Revelation, and expanded to encompass the entire world at the end of this Age.

Without the events of Passover, "Yeshua" (Jesus) would never have been born to Mary who is a direct descendant of King David of the Tribe of Judah—as was prophesied in Isaiah.

> *Isaiah 7:14 "All right then, the Lord himself will choose the sign. Look! The virgin will conceive a child! She will give birth to a son and will call him Emmanuel – 'God is with us."*
>
> *Isaiah 11:1 "There shall come forth out of the stump of Jesse, and a branch shall grow out of his roots. And the spirit of the Lord shall rest upon him......."*
>
> *Isaiah 11:10 "In that day the root of Jesse shall stand as an ensign to the peoples, him shall the nations seek, and his dwellings shall be glorious." (NIV)*

Following the day of Pesach (Passover), begins a seven day holiday called the **Feast of Unleavened Bread**. During this time, we eat nothing that contains any leaven or yeast.

Why no leaven or yeast?

Throughout Scripture, leaven is frequently used as a symbol of SIN.

In ancient times, and in many cultures today, a small piece of leaven was used to ferment an entire portion of dough. It was the leaven that caused the dough to rise—**to become puffed up—just as sin[3]** causes us to become puffed up in our own lives. *That's why* during this time we eat no leaven as a way of saying we want to break the sin cycle in our lives.

Jewish people today celebrate the Feast of Unleavened Bread for eight days, and they call both feasts by one name—Passover. Because "Blindness in part has happened to Israel," (Romans 11:25), they do not fully understand the distinction between these two feasts, Unfortunately, most Jewish people today do not know or read their Bibles at all. Those few who do typically read only selected readings on the Sabbath day.

As mentioned previously, there is a third feast day which is incredibly important to help us understand that Jesus is the promised Messiah. Sadly, the rabbis recognized centuries ago that if Jewish people made the connection between the three feasts of the Passover season they would more easily come to believe in Yeshua (Jesus). Therefore, they changed the date of this third feast so that Jews and Gentiles would not be able to make the connection.

Mô-êd Hă-bēk-ū-rēm (מוֹעֵד הַבִּכּוּרִים)

---

[3] This can include false doctrine: "Beware of the leaven of the Pharisees, which is hypocrisy." [Luke 12:1]
And Jesus said unto them, Take heed and beware of the leaven of the Pharisees and Sadducees. [Matthew 16:6]; Luke 12:1)
And he charged them, saying, Take heed, beware of the leaven of the Pharisees and the leaven of Herod. [Mark 8:15]
"Your glorying is not good. Know ye not that a little leaven leaveneth the whole lump? [1Corinthians 5:6]
Ye were running well; who hindered you that ye should not obey the truth? This persuasion came not of him that calleth you. A little leaven leaveneth the whole lump. [Galatians 5:7-9]

This third feast, the Feast of First Fruits is found in Leviticus 23:9-12. Here The Lord spoke to Moses and told him,

> "Speak to the children of Israel and say to them. When you come into the land which I give unto you, you shall reap the harvest and bring a sheaf of First-Fruits unto the priest....and the day after the Sabbath the priest will wave it and you shall offer a burnt lamb without blemish to the Lord."
> *(Paraphrased from JPS[4] for brevity)*

The exact date of the Feast of First Fruits is then established in the Book of Joshua 5:10-11 as the day after the Sabbath after the Passover. Since Passover fell on the Sabbath in the year in which Jesus was crucified; the Feast of First Fruits was the first day of the week. Jesus was resurrected on the feast of First Fruits as a foreshadowing of our future resurrection in him.

> "But in fact Christ has been raised from the dead, the firstfruits of those who have fallen asleep." (1 Corinthians 15:20)

On that Sunday morning, when the priest was to offer the First Fruits offering in the Temple, Messiah arose from the dead, the first fruits of them that slept (I Cor. 15:20, 23).

The *Regulations* for Firstfruits (Lev. 23:9-14)[5]:
- A sheaf of barley is to be brought to the priest at the Temple. He waves the sheaf before the Lord for acceptance[6].

---

[4] Jewish Publication Society version of the Bible
[5] Adapted from: http://oncedelivered.net/2008/05/29/jesus-in-the-feasts-of-israel-the-feast-of-firstfruits/

- Accompanying sacrifices are to be brought as well: an unblemished male lamb of the first year, a drink offering of wine, and a meal offering of the barley flour mixed with olive oil.
- The people are forbidden to use any part of the harvest in any way until after they offer their firstfruits to the Lord.

The *Ritual* for Firstfruits (Deut. 26:11):
- Firstfruits is to be observed, "When you enter the land the Lord your God is giving you as an inheritance …" (v. 1).
- The firstfruits are to be brought to the priest and the giver is to say, "Today I acknowledge to the Lord your God that I have entered the land the Lord swore to our fathers to give us" (v. 3).
- The priest takes the firstfruits and places them before the altar at the tabernacle (later the Temple), and the giver recites the story of God's deliverance of the Jews from Egypt and the giving of the Promised Land (vv. 4-10).
- The giver then bows down and worships the Lord (v. 10).
- The giver joins the priest and even the foreign resident among the people in rejoicing in all the good things the Lord has given him and his household (v. 11).

Also of interest, Yeshua rose from the dead on what is known as the Havdallah service (meaning *Separation*), the celebration of the end of the Sabbath on Saturday evening. In Jewish tradition, this is known as Messiah's Service, when the following verses of the Bible are read as part of the ceremony (KJV):

---

[6] Catholics today call this the "sign of the cross"

> Behold, God is my salvation; I will trust, and will not be afraid: for God the Lord is my strength and song, and he is become my salvation (Isaiah 12:2-3).
>
> Therefore, with joy shall ye draw water out of the wells of salvation (Psalm 3:9).
>
> Salvation belongeth unto the Lord: thy blessing be upon thy people (Selah. The Hebrew word Selah in this sense is a break in the recital to emphasize the preceding words, similar to Amen). The Lord of Hosts is with us; the God of Jacob is our refuge (Selah) (Psalm 46:12).
>
> The Jews had light and joy and gladness and honor (So be it with us) (Esther 8:16).
>
> I will lift the cup of salvation, and call upon the Name of the Lord (Psalm 116:13).

Before continuing with the teaching about Yeshua and the Passover, permit me to tie these three feasts together (Passover, Unleavened Bread, First Fruits), with the fourth spring feast. Going back to Leviticus 23, continuing from verse 15, God instructs Moses to tell the children of Israel to count seven weeks from the day after Passover (that is the from Feast of First Fruits) and present another wave offering. In Hebrew, this Feast is Shavuot (חג השבועות). In English, we all know it as Pentecost—the day in which Jesus sent His Holy Spirit.

For forty ensuing days[7], the Lord appeared to His disciples in His resurrection body[8], and then ascended into Heaven. Ten days later, the Sunday of the Feast of Pentecost (in Hebrew, Shavuot), the Holy Spirit descended upon the believers in Jerusalem[9] and created the ekklesia, the called out body of Messiah, the church. These fulfillments were obviously no coincidence, but were part of the overall plan and purpose of God in verifying the powerful meaning of the death and resurrection of Messiah and the establishment of the new body of believers.

From then on, the Jewish believers in Messiah undoubtedly informed the people of Israel about the nature of the fulfillment of Passover, First Fruits and Pentecost. It must have made a great impact on the Jewish people who lived between the resurrection of Messiah and the destruction of the Temple in 70 AD, a span of about forty years.

Shavuot, the Feast of Weeks, was held at the beginning of wheat harvesting, seven weeks from the Feast of Firstfruits (Leviticus 23:15-16). This festival commemorated the giving of the Ten Commandments which took place fifty days after the Sabbath following the Passover. On that day God Himself had come down in a cloud onto Mt. Sinai in fire, and smoke, and a blast of God's trumpet, to establish His covenant with His people. Shavuot is therefore commemorated as the birth date of the nation of Israel. At that time three-thousand people died because of their sin (Exodus 32:28).

---

[7] Acts 1:3
[8] Matthew 27:52-53 mentions that many old testament saints also rose from the dead
"[52] ...and the graves were opened; and many bodies of the saints who had fallen asleep were raised; [53] and coming out of the graves after His resurrection, they went into the holy city and appeared to many."
[9] Acts 2:1-13

Fast forward with me a few thousand years.

The cross had met the Law's demand for justice, fulfilling it. Fifty days later, the remaining disciples were gathered together in one place, during the feast of the celebration of the giving of the Ten Commandments. The disciples were commanded to tarry at Jerusalem "for the promise of the Father" (Acts 1:4). Suddenly, once more, as in the days of Sinai, with a mighty rushing wind, tongues of fire and other demonstrations of the Holy Spirit, God established a New Covenant with His people. Whereas before, the Divine Mandate had been carved into tablets of stone, now the Divine Presence took root in hearts of flesh. Whereas before, the Lord empowered Moses to speak as His representative, now Peter took that mantle under the power of the Spirit.[10]

On the day of Pentecost following Jesus' liftoff into Heaven (Acts 2), a new revelation was given to the people of Israel in the gospel preached by the apostles, with the invitation to everyone—both Jewish and Gentile—to enter into a covenant with God through baptism[11] into Messiah.

> Acts 2:38, "Then Peter said unto them, Repent, and be baptized every one of you in the name of Jesus Messiah for the remission of sins, and ye shall receive the gift of the Holy Ghost."

It is more than likely that the two loaves of bread that were brought to the temple and waved before God by the priest on Shavuot represented both Jew and Gentile.

---

[10] Adapted from http://tehanna.com/pentecost/
[11] See *The Baptism of Jesus from a Jewish Perspective*, by Tov Rose, published 2014 for a complete teaching on how the Body of Messiah is made ONE through Jesus' baptism.

"For he is our peace, who hath made both (Jew and Gentile) one, and have broken down the middle wall of partition between us...to make in himself of two (Jew and Gentile) one new man, so making peace" (Ephesians 2:14-15).

Whereas before, Moses had enunciated an offer for reconciliation, now Peter boomed forth a similar cry, and three-thousand people were saved:

> "And with many other words he bore witness and continued to exhort them, saying, "Save yourselves from this crooked generation." So those who received his word were baptized, and there were added that day about three thousand souls." (Acts 2:40-41)

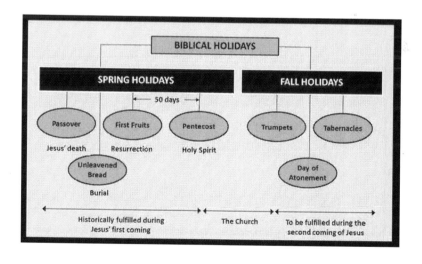

The Passover Seder

בְּדִיקַת חָמֵץ

Bedikat Chametz

In a traditional Jewish household, the woman of the home can spend up to six weeks removing all the cakes, cookies, breads, cereals, baking soda, and anything else that has leaven in it from the house. One might say that, spring cleaning started with the Passover Celebration, and is a Jewish ritual. It is tradition that the wife leaves a small portion of leaven somewhere in the house so that the man of the house can find it and declare the house clean.

According to Jewish tradition, it is the man who has spiritual authority for his household before the Lord. Traditionally, the following strange cleaning tools are used by the man to "clean" his house.

- A Feather
- A Wooden Spoon
- A linen cloth
- and a fire

Leaven represents sin, it cannot be touched, and so the husband picks up the feather and the napkin and searches for the leaven. When the leaven is located, he sweeps it into the wooden spoon, wraps it up in the linen cloth and takes it down to the center of the synagogue courtyard and tosses it into a large raging fire. Upon returning home, he now blesses the house by saying:

> "Now I have purged my home of all leaven!" But just to be certain, he adds "May all manner of leaven which I have neither seen nor removed be considered – null—and—void—and as the dust of the earth. Amen!

Officially, the house has been cleansed. The home is now ready for the Passover celebration.

The ancient Israeli's were instructed to eat the Passover meal ready to go at a moment's notice. Today we relax and recline on pillows. In ancient Middle Eastern societies, only the free could recline at dinner. Today we are free because we are redeemed and thus we recline.

Ceremonial Garments

On Passover, the head of the household puts on a ceremonial garment. He wears a white robe called a כתנ (Kittle), because in Jewish tradition, white is the color of royalty. Jewish men often cover their heads as a sign of respect before God (Exodus 29:6 and Leviticus 8:9). However, instead of wearing the traditional Yarmulke or keepah, the head of the house wears a linen Miter, reflecting the clothing of the High Priest of Israel. He is dressed in Royal robes and a crown, because the head of the household is a king.

The Passover Seder

"**Seder**" (סדר) is a Hebrew word meaning "**order**" because the Passover celebration follows a specific order of service. That order is recorded here in this book called a Haggadah (הגדה), which means "Telling."

There is a customary greeting proclaimed at Passover:

"Let all who are hungry come and eat."

In Jewish tradition, the head of the house is responsible to find people to share the Passover with he and his family; people who have nowhere else to celebrate it. Passover was never just about Jewish people. It has, from its inception, been about all people, Jews and Gentiles, worshipping God together. The very first Passover included approximately 600,000 Egyptians who had seen the judgments on their land and decided to worship the God of Israel (Exodus 12:38)!

Lighting of the Candles

The woman of the house covers her head and lights the candles reciting the following blessing:

אֲשֶׁר קָדְשָׁנוּ בְּמִצְוֹתָיו וְצִוָּנוּ
בָּרוּךְ אַתָּה יְיָ אֱלֹהֵינוּ
וְצִוָּנוּ לְהַדְלִיק נֵר שֶׁל פֶּסַח

Baruch atah Adonai elohenu melech ha'olam, asher kid'shanu b'mitzvoh tov vitzivanu l'khadlik ner shel Pesach -

Blessed art though, O Lord our God, King of the universe who sanctifies us with His commandments, as we light the Passover candles.

Lighting the candles has become an important part of most Jewish festivals as celebrated today. It is a reminder of the eternal light that once burned bright in the Holy Temple. That light was aptly named "Messiah's Light" by some rabbis.

Although the lighting of the candles is a rabbinical practice, it's appropriate that a woman kindles these lights, because it reminds us that the Messiah—the Light of the World (John 8:28)—would come not from the seed of man, but from the seed of woman. The prophet Isaiah foretold, "Behold a virgin shall conceive and bear a son, and she shall call His name Emmanuel—a light to the gentiles and the glory of thy people Israel." (Isaiah 7:14 KJV)

The Traditional Washing of the hands

Urchatz

Ancient Rabbinic regulations require that hands must be washed before dipping food into liquid. In the days when the Temple was standing, it was part of the process of purification to be holy unto the Lord. The purification process also included sacrifice, because no amount of water could cleanse us from our sins. God said "It is blood that makes atonement and without the shedding of blood there is no forgiveness" (Leviticus 17:11; Hebrews 9:22). At this time, we all wash our hands by dipping into the water.

Do you remember the man from Luke 22 who was carrying a pitcher of water? That man that the two Disciples of Jesus were to follow into his house? In the tradition of the day, that man would have been coming from the pool of Siloam, but where the "holy water" that was used in temple rituals was drawn. And water being poured out in the Old Testament often represents the Spirit of God bring poured out on God's people. Keep this in mind as you read what comes next.

It was at this point in the Passover ritual that Yeshua (Jesus) took off his clothes except his underwear, and proceeded to wash his Disciples feet (**John 13:1-17**).

> [1]Now before the Feast of the Passover, when Jesus knew that his hour had come to depart out of this world to the Father, having loved his own who were in the world, he loved them to the end. [2] During supper, when the devil had already put it into the heart of Judas Iscariot, Simon's son, to betray him, [3] Jesus, knowing that the Father had given all things into his hands, and that he had come from God and was going back to God, [4] rose from supper. He laid aside his outer garments, and taking a towel, tied it round his waist. [5] Then he poured water into a basin and began to wash the disciples' feet and to wipe them with the towel that was wrapped round him. [6] He came to Simon Peter, who said to him, "Lord, do you wash my feet?" [7] Jesus

answered him, "What I am doing you do not understand now, but afterwards you will understand." ⁸ Peter said to him, "You shall never wash my feet." Jesus answered him, "If I do not wash you, you have no share with me." ⁹ Simon Peter said to him, "Lord, not my feet only but also my hands and my head!" ¹⁰ Jesus said to him, "The one who has bathed does not need to wash, except for his feet,[a] but is completely clean. And you[b] are clean, but not every one of you." ¹¹ For he knew who was to betray him; that was why he said, "Not all of you are clean."

¹² When he had washed their feet and put on his outer garments and resumed his place, he said to them, "Do you understand what I have done to you? ¹³ You call me Teacher and Lord, and you are right, for so I am. ¹⁴ If I then, your Lord and Teacher, have washed your feet, you also ought to wash one another's feet. ¹⁵ For I have given you an example, that you also should do just as I have done to you. ¹⁶ Truly, truly, I say to you, a servant[c] is not greater than his master, nor is a messenger greater than the one who sent him. ¹⁷ If you know these things, blessed are you if you do them. (ESV)

By washing his Disciples' feet Yeshua was fulfilling a verse in the Old Testament, he was preparing his Disciples to proclaim the Gospel message to every nation on earth (Acts 1:8)!

"How beautiful upon the mountains are the feet of him that bringeth good tidings, that publisheth peace; that bringeth good tidings of good, that publisheth salvation; that saith unto Zion, Thy God reigneth!" (Isaiah 52:7 KJV)[12]

> If there are multiple tables, at this time we need to designate a man at each table to be in charge. We will give this man a title. We'll call him a Shammish (Servant).

(Shammish's bring the ceremonial water to the participants to at least wash their hands)

Explanation of the Four Cups

Passover isn't just a meal, it's a celebration. During this celebration each adult will drink from their cup and refill it three more times.

- The first cup is called the **Kiddush Cup**, or the Cup Sanctification.
- The second cup is called the **Judgment Cup** or the Cup of Plagues.
- The third cup is called the **Cup of The Covenant (some call it the Cup of Redemption or Salvation)**

---

[12] See also Nahum 1:15

which is the focal point of the entire celebration. This is the cup after the meal.
- The <u>fourth</u> cup is called the **Cup of Hallel**, or the Cup of Praise or Joy

With the first cup, the **Kiddush Cup**, the head of the household offers a blessing.

> *The wine used at Passover is sweet red wine.* The wine symbolizes the blood of the lambs that were slain so that our Israeli ancestors could be saved. *It also represents the blood which was shed for <u>our</u> <u>redemption</u> from sin.*

Sin. Nearly all of us have read of the man called Nicodemus, a Pharisee (John 3). He snuck out in the middle of the night because he knew that Jesus was with God; and he wanted to ask him about it, and Jesus told him he couldn't enter the Kingdom of Heaven unless he was Born Again.

Let's look at it:

> "Now there was a man of the Pharisees named Nicodemus, a ruler of the Jews. [2] This man came to Jesus[a] by night and said to him, "Rabbi, we know that you are a teacher come from God, for no one can do these signs that you do unless God is with him." [3] Jesus answered him, "Truly, truly, I say to you, unless one is born again[b] he cannot see the kingdom of God." [4] Nicodemus said to him, "How can a

man be born when he is old? Can he enter a second time into his mother's womb and be born?" ⁵ Jesus answered, "Truly, truly, I say to you, unless one is born of water and the Spirit, he cannot enter the kingdom of God. ⁶ That which is born of the flesh is flesh, and that which is born of the Spirit is spirit.[c] ⁷ Do not marvel that I said to you, 'You[d] must be born again.' ⁸ The wind[e] blows where it wishes, and you hear its sound, but you do not know where it comes from or where it goes. So it is with everyone who is born of the Spirit."

⁹ Nicodemus said to him, "How can these things be?" ¹⁰ Jesus answered him, "Are you the teacher of Israel and yet you do not understand these things? ¹¹ Truly, truly, I say to you, we speak of what we know, and bear witness to what we have seen, but you[f] do not receive our testimony. ¹² If I have told you earthly things and you do not believe, how can you believe if I tell you heavenly things? ¹³ No one has ascended into heaven except he who descended from heaven, the Son of Man.[g] ¹⁴ And as Moses lifted up the serpent in the wilderness, so must the Son of Man be lifted up, ¹⁵ that whoever believes in him may have eternal life.[h]"¹³

---

¹³ • John 3:2 Greek *him*
◻ John 3:3 Or *from above*; the Greek is purposely ambiguous and can mean both *again* and *from above*; also verse 7
◻ John 3:6 The same Greek word means both *wind* and *spirit*
◻ John 3:7 The Greek for *you* is plural here
◻ John 3:8 The same Greek word means both *wind* and *spirit*
◻ John 3:11 The Greek for *you* is plural here; also four times in verse 12

How could Yeshua say that Nicodemus should have understood what he was saying? Nicodemus, a leader in the Israeli Parliament of the day, wasn't just a politician. He was also a teacher in Israel who should have understood the "Born Again" concept.

Here is what Nicodemus should have understood: If you were a sinner during the Temple period, you had to offer a sin offering for yourself if you wanted to be free from sin and have a right relationship with God. If you were a rich person, you offered a bull for the sacrifice. If you were really poor, you offered two turtledoves and two young pigeons like Jesus' mother, Mary did after he was born, according to the Law (see Leviticus 4:1-5:13; 6:24-30; Leviticus 12:8; 14:22; Luke 2:24).

Once the sinner had the proper sacrifice they would afford, they entered the Temple, were ritually purified by being baptized in water (called a Mikvah), which is a symbol of the Holy Spirit washing the sinner. They then offered the sacrifice to the priest. The priest would make certain that the animal was "without spot or blemish" (Exodus 12:5, Leviticus 1:3; 1 Peter 1:19; 2 Peter 3:14; Ephesians 5:27), or in other words, the perfect picture of a *sinless life*.

Next, the sinner laid their right hand on the animal's head while confessing their sins, thus transferring their sins to the animal. This meant that the animal had now become that person's sin! Because the penalty for sin is death, the animal had to die. In return, the animal's sinless life was transferred to and covered the person presenting the sacrifice.

This is called being "Born Again."

☐ John 3:13 Some manuscripts add *who is in heaven*
☐ John 3:15 Some interpreters hold that the quotation ends at verse 15

The sacrifice was good as long as the person remained sinless. Once the person sinned again, another sacrifice needed to be offered. However, Yeshua fulfilled this "being Born Again!" Because if you, as a sinner, were to symbolically lay your hand on the head of the sinless sacrifice named Yeshua (Jesus), confess your sins to the "Lamb of God who takes away the sin of the world," then he becomes your sin sacrifice! And his eternal sinless life comes into you and you live—Born Again—forever with him and His Father in eternity!

(Shammish's fill the first cup—the Kiddish Cup)

THE FIRST CUP

The Blessing

אֱלֹהֵינוּ מֶלֶךְ הָעוֹלָם בּוֹרֵא פְּרִי הַגָּפֶן:
בָּרוּךְ אַתָּה יְיָ

Baruch atah Adonai elohenu melech ha'olam, boei p'ri ha gafin. Amen!

Blessed art thou, O Lord our God, King of the universe, who created the fruit of the vine, Amen.

Everyone Drinks the First Cup

The Service Has Now Begun - The youngest child now comes forward to ask the meaning of Passover.

- *This responsibility falls to the youngest child as a way of guaranteeing teaching and remembrance to future generations, as instructed in Exodus 12:14:*

  > *"This day shall be for you a memorial day, and you shall keep it a <u>feast of the Lord</u>; throughout your generations you shall observe it as an <u>ordinance forever</u>."*

There are two key phrases in this Scripture "feast of the Lord" and "ordinance forever." We are all instructed to *keep this feast, not just the Jewish people, because this is The Lord's Feast!*

The Child asks a Question:

מַה נִּשְׁתַּנָּה הַלַּיְלָה הַזֶּה מִכָּל הַלֵּילוֹת?

(Ma Nishtanah Halailaw Hazeh Meekowl Halaylot ?)

"Why is this night different from all other nights?"

It is the responsibility of the Head of the House to respond by telling the Story of Passover along with saying, "This night is different because of what God did for ME. When he brought Me out of the Egypt with His mighty arm and His strong hand—when He delivered ME from the house of bondage!"

We are supposed to take the story of Passover personally, as though each and every one of us has gone through it. It isn't supposed to be just a story about our ancestors, but a personally adopted group communal experience that we have all participated in and experienced, that has changed us and brought us closer to our Maker.

The Maggid

מַגִּיד

(Recounting the Exodus Story)

We are told to remember the Passover story all the days of our lives, and to take the story of Passover personally:

> "And this day shall be unto you for a memorial; and ye shall keep it a feast to the LORD throughout your generations; ye shall keep it a feast by an ordinance for ever."
> *(Exodus 12:14)*

The Jewish sages of old have said that this is all encompassing Holy season that includes days and nights, and extends beyond this world into the next –which includes the time of the Messiah Yeshua (Jesus).

Leader: *Blessed is God, who gave the Torah (instructions) to His people Israel. Blessed is He, and Blessed is God the Father who sent His only son for our Yeshua (Salvation).*

The Talmud[14] **speaks about four sons and how the Head the House is supposed to respond to them concerning this first question:** These four sons are 1) One who is **"wise;"** and 2) one who is **"contrary;"** 3) one who is **"simple;"** and 4) one who **"can't form a question."** *(Talmud (Pesachim 114b) teaching taken from Deut. 6:20-25)*[15]

> [20] "When your son asks you in time to come, 'What is the meaning of the testimonies and the statutes and the rules that the LORD our God has commanded you?' [21] then you shall

---

[14] The **Talmud** is the written form of that which, in the time of Jesus, was called the Traditions of the Elders, and to which He makes frequent allusions. The **Talmud** (/ˈtɑːlmʊd, -məd, ˈtæl-/; Hebrew: תַּלְמוּד *talmūd* "instruction, learning", from a root *lmd* "teach, study") is a central text of Rabbinic Judaism. It is also traditionally referred to as **Shas** (ש״ס), a Hebrew abbreviation of *shisha sedarim*, the "six orders". The term "Talmud" normally refers to the Babylonian Talmud, though there is also an earlier collection known as the Jerusalem Talmud.

The Talmud has two components. The first part is the Mishnah (Hebrew: משנה, c. 200 CE), the written compendium of Judaism's Oral Torah (Torah meaning "Instruction", "Teaching" in Hebrew). The second part is the Gemara (c. 500 CE), an elucidation of the Mishnah and related Tannaitic writings that often ventures onto other subjects and expounds broadly on the Hebrew Bible. The term *Talmud* can be used to mean either the Gemara alone, or the Mishnah and Gemara as printed together.

The whole Talmud consists of 63 tractates, and in standard print is over 6,200 pages long. It is written in Tannaitic Hebrew and Aramaic. The Talmud contains the teachings and opinions of thousands of rabbis on a variety of subjects, including Halakha (law), Jewish ethics, philosophy, customs, history, lore and many other topics. The Talmud is the basis for all codes of Jewish law and is much quoted in rabbinic literature.

[15] Although most haggadah's reference this story to Deuteronomy 6:20-25, it is actually a paraphrase and teaching from Deuteronomy. The actual story—in context—came from the Jerusalem Talmud *Pesachim 114b*.

say to your son, 'We were Pharaoh's slaves in Egypt. And the LORD brought us out of Egypt with a mighty hand. ²² And the LORD showed signs and wonders, great and grievous, against Egypt and against Pharaoh and all his household, before our eyes. ²³ And he brought us out from there, that he might bring us in and give us the land that he swore to give to our fathers. ²⁴ And the LORD commanded us to do all these statutes, to fear the LORD our God, for our good always, that he might preserve us alive, as we are this day.²⁵ And it will be righteousness for us, if we are careful to do all this commandment before the LORD our God, as he has commanded us.' *Deut. 6:20-25*

The "Sons" can also represent people groups and how they respond to the story of Salvation.

1) **The wise son asks:** "What is the meaning of the rules, laws and customs which the Eternal our God has commanded us?" You shall explain to him the laws of Passover, to the smallest detail, and don't forget to tell him about the Afikomen (that which is resurrected later).

2) **The contrary son asks**: "What is the meaning of this service to **you**?" The rabbis tell us that because he excluded himself, that we should exclude him from the

story of the Israeli's redemption from slavery in Egypt.[16]

3) **The simple son asks**: "What is this?" he says. To him you shall say: "With a strong hand, God brought us out of Egypt, from the house of bondage." To our sons and daughters we say, "Through grace, our Messiah took us by the hand and led us away from bondage to sin."

4) As for **the son who couldn't form a question**, the rabbis say, you must say; as it is written in the Bible, "You shall tell your child on that day: This is done because of that which God did for me when I came forth out of Egypt." And I say, through the grace of Our Lord Yeshua (Jesus), and the price He paid on Calvary, we have eternal life.

The traditional story of Passover does not begin with God's redemption of the children of Israel, out of the land of Egypt. It begins: "Long, long ago our forefathers were worshipers of idols. Now the Eternal is our God and we worship Him." The Bible tells us: "And Joshua said to all the people: Thus said the Eternal God of Israel: In the days of old, your forefathers lived beyond the river; that is

---

[16] Many worldly people exclude themselves (much like this boy) from our personal stories of our redemption from sin, through the messiah Yeshua. We, as believers cannot afford to lose one soul to the adversary. The rabbi's tell the Jewish fathers to deny the son the opportunity for redemption, and to keep it to himself. This goes contrary to the teaching of the Yshua (*Matthew 26*). I sincerely hope that you will not take the advice of the rabbi's and sages of old!

Terah the father of Abraham and Nahor. They worshipped other Gods. Then I took Abraham, your father, from beyond the rivers. I led him through the whole land of Canaan. Then I increased his family by giving him a son, Isaac. And I gave to Isaac two sons, Jacob, who I call Israel, and Esau. To Esau I gave Mount Seir as a possession, but Jacob and his sons I sent down to Egypt."[17]

Blessed is God, who keeps His promise to Israel, blessed is He. For God foretold the end of the bondage to Abraham at the Covenant of Sacrifices *(Gen 15:3)*. For God said to Abraham: "Know you that your children will be strangers in a land not their own. They will be enslaved there and will be oppressed four hundred years. The nation who will oppress them shall however be judged. Afterward they will come forth with great wealth."

Pour and Raise the cup of wine and say:

This promise made to our forefathers also holds true for us. More than once our enemies have risen to destroy us. In every generation they rise against us and seek our

---

[17] See also Malachi 1:1-5: " **1** This is a divine revelation. The LORD spoke his word to Israel through Malachi.
2 "I loved you," says the LORD.
"But you ask, 'How did you love us?'
"Wasn't Esau Jacob's brother?" declares the LORD. "I loved Jacob, **3** but Esau I hated. I turned his mountains into a wasteland and left his inheritance to the jackals in the desert.
4 "The descendants of Esau may say, 'We have been beaten down, but we will rebuild the ruins.'
"Yet, this is what the LORD of Armies says: They may rebuild, but I will tear it down. They will be called 'the Wicked Land' and 'the people with whom the LORD is always angry.' **5** You will see these things with your own eyes and say, 'Even outside the borders of Israel the LORD is great.'"

destruction. But the Holy One, blessed be He, saves us from their hands.

Put down the cup and continue:

Come and learn what Laban the Syrian tried to do to our father Jacob. While Pharaoh decreed only against the males, Laban desired to uproot all of us *(Gen 29-31)*. For it is written:" A Syrian sought to destroy my father; and he went down to Egypt and dwelled there, a handful, few in number. There he became a nation, great, mighty and numerous."

This section (The Maggid) is the recounting of the miracles which God performed as He brought the Children of Israel out of bondage in Egypt. As we recap these events recorded in Exodus, we are told again, to take it personally. (Ex 12:14)

Reader response: Repeat the words in BOLD after the reader.

Jacob and his family **"went down to Egypt"** *(Repeat after the reader)* – Why did he go down to Egypt? He was compelled by God's decree because of famine in the Land of Canaan. (Gen 46:3-4)

"He dwelt there" *(Repeat)* — Jacob the father of the Children of Israel did not go down to Egypt to settle there, but only to stay for a short while. Scripture tells us "And they said to Pharaoh, we have come to dwell in the land because there is no pasture for the flocks of your servants, since the famine is very bad in the land of Canaan; and now let your servants dwell in the land of Goshen." (Gen 47:4)

"Few in number" *(Repeat)* — Scripture tells us seventy souls went down into Egypt (Gen 46:27), and "God has made you as numerous as the stars in heaven." (Deut 1:10)

"He became a nation" *(Repeat)* — We learn that Israel became a distinct nation in Egypt. (Ex. 1:7)

"Great and mighty" *(Repeat)* — The children of Israel were fruitful and increased and multiplied and became very strong and numerous, so the land was full of them. (Ex. 1:7)"

"And numerous" *(Repeat)* — The Lord God multiplied the Children if Israel (Deut. 1:10) Ezekiel writes, "I have caused you to multiply like the bud of the field, and you are grown, and are great; and you come in the finest ornaments. Your breasts are formed, yet you were naked and bare." (Ezk. 16:7) JPSV

The Egyptians did evil unto The Children of Israel and they made them suffer. They set upon them hard work.

It is recorded in the Bible: "Come, we must deal shrewdly with them or they will become even more numerous and, if war breaks out, will join our enemies, fight against us and leave the country." (Ex 1:10) NIV

"And they made us suffer" (Repeat) — As the Bible relates: "So the Egyptians set taskmasters over them in order to oppress them with their burdens; and they built Pithom and Ramses as store cities for Pharaoh." (Ex 1:11)

"And they set us upon hard work" (Repeat) — As the Bible states: "And Egypt made the children of Israel labor rigorously."

"So we cried unto God, (Repeat) — *the God of our fathers, (Repeat)* — *and God heard our voice," (Repeat)* — and He remembered His covenant with Abraham, with Isaac and with Jacob."

He saw our affliction (Repeat) — as it is written: "And God saw the children of Israel, and God understood their plight."

He saw our burden (Repeat) — this recalls the drowning of the male children, as it is said: "Every son that is born, you shall cast into the Nile, but every daughter you may keep alive."

He saw our oppression." (Repeat) — This refers to crushing our lives, as the Bible says: "And I have seen the oppression with which the Egyptians are oppressing them."

"And God brought us forth from Egypt, (Repeat) with a strong hand, (Repeat) and with an outstretched arm, (Repeat) and with great terror, (Repeat) and signs, (Repeat) and wonders." (Repeat)

Not by a ministering angel, (Repeat)** — **not by a fiery angel, (Repeat)** — **not by a messenger, (Repeat)** — **but by Himself, (Repeat) — in His glory, did the Holy One of Israel, blessed be He did all this As the Bible records: "And I will pass through the land of Egypt on that night, and I will smite all the first-born in the land of Egypt, from man to beast, and against all the gods of Egypt I will execute judgments. It is I, the Eternal." (Ex 12:12)

"And I will pass through the land of Egypt (Repeat)** — **I and not a ministering angel; (Repeat) —"and I will smite the first-born in the land of Egypt"—***I and not a fiery angel; (Repeat)*** — and against all the gods of Egypt I will execute judgments"—***I and not a messenger; (Repeat)*** — ***"I the Eternal" (Repeat)** — **I and no other. (Repeat)***

"With a strong hand" *(Repeat)* — This refers to the cattle plague, as it is said in the Bible: "Behold, the hand of the Eternal will be against the cattle that is in the field, against the horses, the donkeys, the camels, the oxen and the sheep, a very grievous plague." (Ex 9:3)

"And with an outstretched arm" *(Repeat)* — Scripture states, "So I will stretch out my hand and strike the Egyptians with all the wonders that I will perform among them." (Ex 3:19-20)

"And with great terror" *(Repeat)* — This refers to the Revelation of God to Israel, as it is said: "Has any God ever tried to go and remove one nation from the midst of another nation, with trials, with signs and with wonders, and with battle, and with a strong hand and outstretched arm, and with great terrors, as all that the Eternal your God did for you in Egypt before your eyes?" (Deut 4:34)

"And with signs" *(Repeat)* — this refers to the rod of Moses, as it is written: "And thou, Moses, shalt take in thy hand this rod wherewith thou shalt do the signs." (Ex 4:17)

"And wonders" *(Repeat)* — This refers to the plague of blood; the slaying of the first born; the dividing of the sea; allowing us to pass through on dry ground; drowning our oppressors; guiding us for forty years in the wilderness; feeding us manna; giving us the Sabbath; bringing us to Mount Sinai; giving us Torah (The law); bringing us to The Land of Milk and Honey; giving us the Ark of the Covenant.

As recorded in Scripture; "He rescues and he saves; He performs signs and wonders in the heavens and on the earth." (Dan 6:7)

Redemption is the very heart of Passover.

Passover is not just God's message of redemption. It describes God's **means** of redemption through the sacrifice of a Passover lamb. The Children of Israel were instructed to take a spotless lamb, to keep it in their house for four days; and then to kill it, roast it whole without breaking any of its bones, and to apply its blood to the door posts of

their homes (Ex 12:3-11). According to tradition, the blood was applied to the lintel using Hyssop. Because of their obedience to God's command, their faith in the effectiveness of His provision; my ancestors were spared the horror of the tenth and final plague that fell upon the people of Egypt. When the LORD God saw the blood on the door posts, Death was forced to **PASS OVER** (to state the obvious, this is the origin of the name of the holiday, **Passover.** In Hebrew, it is called Pesach.). The celebration today was designed by the Pharisees/Rabbis beginning 2000 years ago to commemorate the time when death passed over the houses of Israel because of the blood of the innocent Passover lamb. The symbols of Passover were designed to by physical reminders of the story elements to aid us in teaching the story to our children.

As believers in Jesus, the story and elements should remind us of an even greater redemption through the sacrifice of another Passover Lamb, the Messiah Yeshua (Jesus). None of the bones of those first Passover lambs were broken. In the same way, none of Yeshua's bones were broken when he died, even though it was customary to break the legs of men who were crucified this did not happen in Yeshua's case.

At the original Passover, each man had to personally apply the blood of the lamb to his home to show that he had accepted the sacrifice of the lamb as covering and protection from judgment. In the same way, each one of us today must accept the sacrifice of Jesus personally, and claim Him as our own protection from judgment for our sins.

The Child asks the First Question:

שֶׁבְּכָל הַלֵּילוֹת אָנוּ אוֹכְלִין חָמֵץ וּמַצָּה. הַלַּיְלָה

הַזֶּה כֻּלּוֹ מַצָּה?

Shebchawl Halaylot Awnu Ochleen Chawmatz umatza Halailaw hazeh Kulo Matzaw?

Child translates the first question: On all other nights we eat either leavened or unleavened bread, but on this night why do we eat only unleavened bread (matzah)?

Adult answers to the first question: Our ancestors, in their haste to leave Egypt, had to take their bread with them while it was still flat.[18]

---

[18] That night, they are to eat the meat, roasted in the fire; with *matzah* and *maror*.
—Exodus 12:8
From the evening of the fourteenth day of the first month the twenty-first day, you are to eat *matzah*.
—Exodus 12:18
You are not to eat any *hametz* with it; for seven days you are to eat with it *matzah*, the bread of affliction; for you came out of the land of Egypt in haste. Thus you will remember the day you left the land of Egypt as long as you live.
—Deuteronomy 16:3
For six days you are to eat *matzah*; on the seventh day there is to be a festive assembly for JEHOVAH your God; do not do any kind of work.
—Deuteronomy 16:8

(Matzah-Tosh) (מצה תוש) — The head of the household removes the middle layer, and recites a blessing:

בָּרוּךְ אַתָּה יְיָ אֱלֹהֵינוּ מֶלֶךְ הָעוֹלָם הַמּוֹצִיא לֶחֶם מִן הָאָרֶץ.

Baruch atah Adonai elohenu melech ha'olam, ha motshi lechem min ha oritz. Amen.

Blessed art though, O lord our God, King of the Universe, Who has brought forth bread from the earth, Amen.

The head of the household then breaks the middle matzah in two. He sets one half aside, and he gives the other half a special name. The **AFIKOMEN**. Afikomen is a Greek word meaning "that which comes later." The Afikomen isn't eaten now. We will come back to it later in the ceremony. First we wrap it in a white linen cloth—a symbol of burial—and then it's hidden from sight. Only the leader of the Seder knows where the Afikomen is hidden. Later it will have to be brought back, or the service will not be allowed to continue until it is found. The head of the house hides it somewhere and a game of hide-and-seek ensues among the children…but, more about that later.

(THE AFIKOMEN IS NOW HIDDEN SOMEWHERE IN THE HOUSE BY THE HEAD OF THE HOUSE)

The Child asks the Second Question:

שֶׁבְּכָל הַלֵּילוֹת אָנוּ אוֹכְלִין שְׁאָר יְרָקוֹת הַלַּיְלָה הַזֶּה מָרוֹר?

Shebchawl Halaylot Awnu Ochleen Shawr Y'Raukot Halailaw hazeh Maror?

Child translates the second question: On all other nights we eat herbs of any kind; but on this night why do we eat only bitter herbs?

Adult answers the second question: Eating bitter herbs reminds us of the suffering and anguish from which the Lord saved us.[19]

---

[19] Exodus 12:8; Numbers 9:11

The Seder Plate

Despite its appearance, it's not used for deviled eggs. We place a symbolic piece of food from the Passover service in each one of the compartments.

The bitter herbs are one of the three items specifically prescribed by God that were to be eaten during the Passover (Exodus 12:8; Numbers 9:11). Its prominence in the Passover Seder has continued demonstrated by its inclusion on the Seder plate and multiple uses during the Seder. A variety of foods may be used, horseradish, romaine lettuce, and watercress being the most common, but whatever is used, it must be included in the group of plants whose common characteristics are "bitterness, possessing sap, with a graying appearance." (*Gemara*, Pesachim 39a) The manner in which the bitter herbs are served is purely a matter of choice (i.e. – wafer slices or ground horseradish, leaves or shredded lettuce); however, it is felt by some scholars that the bitter herb that is placed on the Seder plate should be whole.[20]

Unlike the other two items prescribed for the original Passover, unleavened bread and the Lamb sacrifice, which have either evolved or been discontinued, the bitter herbs have maintained its significance and meaning. In fact, its involvement in the Seder has actually grown over time.

The bitter herbs are eaten sitting upright, not reclining as in other times of the Seder when wine is partaken or vegetable greens dipped and eaten. The primary reason for this is that slaves were not allowed to recline as the freemen did when they ate their meals. Because the bitter herbs are a reminder of the bitterness of slavery, participants do not recline, but rather assume the position of slaves. In essence this puts the participant in the place of his or her ancestors fulfilling the command contained in the Haggadah, "In every generation each individual is bound to regard himself as if he personally had gone forth from Egypt."

The proper amount of bitter herbs is roughly the equivalent to the bulk of one olive. It is dipped in charoset the first time it is eaten; the second time, it is eaten with charoset in the Hillel Sandwich[21]. This is interpreted to show that the Israelites were able to withstand the bitterness of slavery because they could taste the sweetness of future deliverance and freedom. Thus, some Jewish people, after dipping the bitter herbs in charoset, will shake off the excess so as to

---

[20] Levin, Meyer. *An Israel Haggadah for Passover* (New York: Harry N. Abrams, Inc. Publishers, no date) 30

[21] According to Rabbi Hillel, instead of eating the Passover Lamb today, instead we are to substitute charoset. We take some matzah and smear some maror (horseradish) on one end and some haroset on the other and then top off the matzah with another piece.

simply take the edge off the bitterness rather than equalizing the bitter and the sweet.[22]

The meaning of the bitter herbs is clear. The Mishnah[23] quotes Rabbi Gameliel (1st Century c.e.) of whom Saul of Tarsus was a disciple, explaining that the bitter herbs draw one's attention to the condition of the Israelites in Egypt "because the Egyptians embittered the lives of our fathers in Egypt."[24] Many other authors have pointed to Exodus 1:14 as the scriptural basis of this explanation.

> "And they made their lives bitter with hard service, in mortar and bricks, and in all kinds of work in the field; in all their work they made them serve with rigor."[25]

Over the years, this interpretation has been almost universally accepted and included in the Haggadah.

For Christians who take an interest in Passover, the bitter herbs carry additional significance. Not only does it represent the bitterness of the Israeli's slavery in Egypt, but it may also represent the bitterness experienced by Jesus both in the Garden of Gethsemane and on the cross. Furthermore, for some it can represent the bitter persecution early Christians received at the hands of the Romans until Christianity.. The relief that came from such recognition is comparable in the eyes of Christians to the

---

[22] Davis, Rabbi Avrohom. *The Metsudah Linear Passover Haggadah* (Hoboken: KTAV Publishing House, 1993) 47
[23] an authoritative collection of exegetical material embodying the oral tradition of Jewish law and forming the first part of the Talmud.
[24] *Mishnah*. Pesachim 10:5
[25] Exodus 1:14

relief experienced by the Israeli's when finally released from Egypt.[26]

The Seder Plate Items

1) **Karpas:** The first item on the plate is called **Karpas** (כרפס) or greens. We usually use parsley or lettuce. In ancient times they used Hyssop. We are supposed to dip the Hyssop into salt water which represents tears—the tears we shed in this life and the tears our ancestors shed as slaves in Egypt.

Jesus fulfilled the **Karpas** in John 19:29:

"A jar of sour wine was sitting there, so they soaked a sponge in it, put it on a hyssop branch, and held it up to [Jesus'] lips."[27]

The Child asks the Third Question:

שֶׁבְּכָל הַלֵּילוֹת אֵין אָנוּ מַטְבִּילִין אֲפִילוּ פַּעַם אֶחָת הַלַּיְלָה

הַזֶּה שְׁתֵּי פְעָמִים?

(Shebchawl Halaylot Ayn Awnu Matbeeleen

---

[26] Adapted from http://avirtualpassover.com/maror
[27] A branch of hyssop bore the sponge used to offer vinegar to Yeshua at His crucifixion (John 19:29 ; Matthew 27:48 ; Mark 15:36 mention a reed).

Afeelu Echat paam Halailaw hazeh Sh'tay P'Awmeem?)

The Child recites the Question: On all other nights we do not dip our herbs even once, on this night why do we dip them twice in saltwater?

Adult answers the third question: We dip our herbs which represent life into the saltwater which represents the tears of life to remind us of our life in slavery under Pharaoh in Egypt. So before we eat them we dip them twice to remind us that life without redemption is a life immersed in tears. **(Eat the parsley dipped twice in saltwater)**

(Shammish's pass the parsley and salt water around)

2) **Hatzaret:** (חֲזֶרֶת) the Root of Bitterness.

חֲזֶרֶת - **Hatzaret** is the **root of the bitter herb**, usually a horseradish root. This symbol reminds us that life in this world is filled with bitterness, as it certainly was for the Israeli's in Egypt. As we look at our lives prior to knowing the Yeshua, many of us can relate to a time of bitterness in our own lives, not to mention difficulties that pop up along the way. This is the Root of Bitterness that the author of Hebrews writes about in Hebrews 12: 14-15:

> "¹⁴Follow peace with all men, and holiness, without which no man shall see the Lord: ¹⁵Looking diligently lest any man fail of the grace of God; lest any root of bitterness springing up trouble you, and thereby many be defiled;"

and Paul refers to in Ephesians 4:31:

> *"³¹Let all bitterness, wrath, anger, clamor, and evil speaking be put away from you, with all malice. ³²And be kind to one another, tenderhearted, forgiving one another, even as God in Jesus forgave you" (NIV).*

and Paul refers to in 1 Corinthians 11:30:

> *"That is why many among you are weak and sick, and a number of you have fallen asleep."*

We are not supposed to have bitterness in our congregations and our homes. We are supposed to as much as possible, live at peace with all men[28]. According to Messiah himself, we are supposed to fulfill all the Law and Prophets by obeying the first great commandment and another like it:

> "²⁸And one of the scribes came up and heard them disputing with one another, and seeing that he answered them well, asked him, "Which commandment is the most important of all?" ²⁹Jesus answered, "The most important is, 'Hear, O Israel: The Lord our God, the Lord is one. ³⁰And you shall

---
[28] Romans 12:14-18

> love the Lord your God with all your heart and with all your soul and with all your mind and with all your strength.' ^{31} The second is this: 'You shall love your neighbor as yourself.' There is no other commandment greater than these." ^{32} And the scribe said to him, "You are right, Teacher. You have truly said that he is one, and there is no other besides him. ^{33} And to love him with all the heart and with all the understanding and with all the strength, and to love one's neighbor as oneself, is much more than all whole burnt offerings and sacrifices." ^{34} And when Jesus saw that he answered wisely, he said to him, "You are not far from the kingdom of God." And after that no one dared to ask him any more questions." (Mark 12:28-34 ESV)

As a matter of fact, as believers in Yeshua we are not even allowed to hold onto unforgiveness toward any one at all, or else God will not hear our prayers!

> "And when you pray, you must not be like the hypocrites. For they love to stand and pray in the synagogues and at the street corners, that they may be seen by others. Truly, I say to you, they have received their reward. 6 But when you pray, go into your room and shut the door and pray to your Father who is in secret. And your Father who sees in secret will reward you.

> 7 "And when you pray, do not heap up empty phrases as the Gentiles do, for they think that they will be heard for their many words. 8 Do not be like them, for your Father knows what you need before you ask him. 9 Pray then like this:
> "Our Father in heaven,
> hallowed be your name.
> 10 Your kingdom come,
> your will be done,
> on earth as it is in heaven.
> 11 Give us this day our daily bread,
> 12 and forgive us our debts,
> as we also have forgiven our debtors.
> 13 And lead us not into temptation,
> but deliver us from evil.
> 14 For if you forgive others their trespasses, your heavenly Father will also forgive you, 15 but if you do not forgive others their trespasses, neither will your Father forgive your trespasses." (Matthew 6:5-15 ESV)

Bitterness is a serious thing to God! We're not supposed to retain it, not even when it comes to bitterness toward ourselves, or others. How many of us wouldn't be in relationship with someone who speaks so horribly to you, but you speak even worse inside your own head? This is just another form of idolatry! You're essentially telling God that you are not worthy of the sacrifice that was paid for your salvation; that your opinion is more important than His opinion of you.

The truth is that God has called us while we are still sinners.[29] His opinion of us is what matters and we are not to have bitterness in our lives, whether it is toward ourselves, toward God, or toward others. We should rather be living and rejoicing in the truth of Psalm 133:

> "Behold, how good and pleasant it is
> when brothers dwell in unity![30]
> ² It is like the precious oil on the head,
> running down on the beard,
> on the beard of Aaron,
> running down on the collar of his robes!
> ³ It is like the dew of Hermon,
> which falls on the mountains of Zion!
> For there the LORD has commanded the
> blessing,
> life for evermore."

3) **Maror** (אמור): The Root of Bitterness ground up or sliced.

> We are supposed to eat about a teaspoon of this bitterness on the unleavened bread. This is supposed to make us cry! We are supposed to experience a small taste of the bitterness experienced by our ancestors in Egypt. It was about this dish that Yeshua said,
>
> "Jesus answered, "One who dips his bread in the dish with me will betray me. **24** The Son of Man will die as

---

[29] Romans 5:8-10; 1 John 4:10
[30] Psalm 133:1 Or *dwell together*

the Scriptures say he will, but how terrible for that man who will betray the Son of Man! It would have been better for that man if he had never been born!" **25** Judas, the traitor, spoke up. "Surely, Teacher, you don't mean me?" he asked. Jesus answered, "So you say." **Matthew 26:23-3** (Good News Translation)

(Shammish's break off piece of Matzah and put Maror on it and gives a piece to each person at the table)

4) **Charoset** (חרוסת) (Nuts and Spices). A sweet, crumbly, pebbly, brown mixture that represents the mortar used to make bricks. It is made with chopped walnuts, grated apples, cinnamon, sweet red wine. Raisins and honey are added by some. The rabbis tell us that the bitterest of labor is sweetened with the promise of redemption. The rabbis tell us that the bitterest of labor is sweetened with the promise of redemption. As believers, we have been able to experience this first hand as we grow spiritually in the knowledge that Yeshua (Jesus) is our redeemer.

Charoset represents sweet fellowship and to remind us how God gave sweet freedom in the middle of bitter slavery.

(Shammish's break off another piece of Matzah Distribute and eat both together)

5) The Egg, (**This is not an Easter egg.**) Some refer to this as the **Chagigah** (חגיגה), (The roasted egg) which was the name given to the Daily Temple Sacrifice as a Peace Offering in Jerusalem. We roast the egg, and that turns it brown. In modern Passovers, the Chagigah is a token of grief over the destruction of the second temple in 70 A.D. The egg is broken open, sliced, given out to each person at the table, and then dipped in saltwater, which means what? **Tears.** However, it is not only a token of grief, because it is also a symbol of new life, and thus resurrection.

Some Rabbis teach that there must be two eggs on the Passover plate as Two Witnesses.

(Shammish's Slice and Distribute the egg dipped in salt water)

The Child asks the Fourth Question:

שֶׁבְּכָל הַלֵּילוֹת אָנוּ אוֹכְלִין בֵּין יוֹשְׁבִין וּבֵין מְסֻבִּין.

הַלַּיְלָה הַזֶּה כֻּלָּנוּ מְסֻבִּין?

(Shebchawl Halaylot Awnu Ochleen Beyn Yo'Shaven Uvayn M'Subeen Halailaw hazeh Kulawnu M'Subeen)?

Child reads the fourth question: On all other nights we eat our meals in any manner; on this night why do we sit around the table in a reclining position.

Adult answers the fourth question: We recline tonight because our Seder is being celebrated in Shalom (peace) before the Almighty.

As believers in Jesus—our Messiah—we have rest, peace, and deliverance through our LORD and His Atonement. Jesus and the His Apostles also reclined at their last Seder. Luke wrote about it…

> "When the hour came, Jesus and his apostles reclined at the table. And he said to them, "I have eagerly desired to eat this Passover with you before I suffer."(Luke 22:14-15) (NIV)

6.) The last item on the Seder plate is called the **Z'roah** (זרע). It is the shank bone of the lamb. Passover is also known as the Feast of the Passover Lamb, and yet at a traditional Passover, lamb is not served today. The lambs that used to be eaten at Passover were the Passover Sacrifices. However, in 70 A.D. the Temple in Jerusalem was destroyed, and so was the altar where the sacrifices had been made. For this reason no lamb is served at Passover. Instead the Z'roah, like the egg, the chagigah, reminds us of sacrifices which are no longer offered. The presence of these two elements—the egg and the shank bone—point us to the fact that Jewish people today have no way of having their relationship with God restored, renewed, or their sins forgiven without offering a sacrifice.

Scripture clearly states,

> "For the life of the flesh is in the blood: and I have given it to you upon the altar to make atonement for your souls: for it is the blood that makes an atonement for your souls." (Leviticus 17:11)

Some people might object, yet a clear reading of scripture and every Haggadah at Passover instructs us to take the story of Passover **personally**, as though each one of us were being brought out of Egypt, going through the redemption process. If we're supposed to take the story of redemption personally because each one of us needs to be redeemed, then why are there no sacrifices today? With no temple sacrifice, how is redemption possible? How can we be redeemed?

History and Scripture hold the answer: Two thousand years ago, there lived a Jewish man named Yochannon. You might know him better as John the Baptist. One day, he was performing the baptism (**Mikvah** (מִקְוָה)) of conversion of people coming from a pagan life to becoming Jewish, but performing the ritual on *Jewish* people. He was a very controversial person as well as a prophet of God. The Jewish leadership didn't like that he was baptizing *Jewish people* with the baptism of pagan conversion to Judaism! The traditional ritual took place in the River Jordan, which is where he was one day when his gaze fell upon a man—his cousin—Yeshua (Jesus), and John declared,

> "Behold the Lamb of God Who takes away the sin of the world!" (John 1:29)

Why is this significant?

Jesus did not need to go through this ritual of conversion from paganism to the religion of Israel, but he did so anyway. When his cousin John protested, Jesus explained, that it had to happen this way:

> 13 Then Jesus came from Galilee to the Jordan to be baptized by John. 14 But John tried to deter him, saying, "I need to be baptized by you, and do you come to me?"
> 15 Jesus replied, "Let it be so now; it is proper for us to do this to fulfill all righteousness." Then John consented.
> 16 As soon as Jesus was baptized, he went up out of the water. At that moment heaven was opened, and he saw the Spirit of God descending like a dove and alighting on him.
> 17 And a voice from heaven said, "This is my Son, whom I love; with him I am well pleased." Matthew 3:13-17 (NIV)

Jesus through that ritual baptism was anointed both with water and the Holy Spirit[31]. In doing so, he was the only one in history authorized to become the atonement **not made through the sacrifice of lambs**, but the sacrifice of **The** Passover Lamb, the Lamb of God.

---

[31] Luke 3:22; Matthew 3:16; John 1:32

The Second Cup
It is now time for the second Cup

The Judgment Cup or the Cup of Plagues.

In Jewish tradition, a full cup represents complete joy. But we cannot have complete joy at Passover, because of those in our lives who do not share with us in the redemption story. Traditionally, we are to mourn and express our sorrow for the Egyptians over their loss, as we remember the ten plagues that the Lord brought upon them through the hardening of Pharaoh's heart. Pharaoh repeatedly defied God. He was told what God wanted him to do, but each time he said **"NO I WILL NOT!**

Pharaoh brought death and destruction, not only to his Land, but into his own home! His firstborn son died because of his hardness of heart. Yet, rather than sit in judgment over Pharaoh, we should consider our own hearts: How often do we choose our desires over God's direction? How often do we know God's will for our lives, but still say, no? Let's not be like Pharaoh. Let's ask God to give us tender hearts towards Him and His direction in our lives.

According to tradition, before we drink the second cup, we are supposed to empty some of the contents, as we remove one drop for each plague as we recite them together.

- Blood   -   דָּם   (Dam)
- Frogs   -   צְפַרְדֵּעַ   (Ts'faday-ah)
- Gnats (lice)   -   כִּנִּים   (Kinnim)
- Flies   -   עָרוֹב   (A'rov)
- Pestilence   -   דֶּבֶר   (Dayvayr)
- Boils   -   שְׁחִין   (Sh'chin)
- Hail   -   בָּרָד   (Barad)
- Locust   -   אַרְבֶּה   (Arbay)
- Darkness   -   חֹשֶׁךְ   (Choshech)
- Firstborn Slain - מַכַּת בְּכוֹרוֹת (Makkat B'chorot)

Before we drink this cup, take a few moments to consider those in your life who do not know Messiah. Pray for them that they might have hearts that are not hardened to the message of Yeshua (Jesus)!

(Drink the second cup)

Although Passover is a night of rejoicing and thanksgiving, it is also a serious event during which we consider whether or not our own motivations before God are pure. We have so much to thank God for this day. We thank Him for the miracles He performed at Passover and for delivering His people from bondage. We also thank Him for delivering us from our own slavery to sin. Let's rejoice in the freedom He has given us in Messiah Jesus!

Dayenu: There is a traditional chant and song that is always sung before the meal. It's audience participation.

Da-yenu which means "**It is Enough**"

Reader   **Response:** *Da-Yenu!*

Had He only brought us out of Egypt.
Had He only judged the Egyptians.
Had He only destroyed their gods.
Had He only slain their first born.
Had He only given us riches.
Had He only divided the sea to let us pass thru
Had He only sank our foe into the depths.
Had He only supplied our needs for forty years.
Had He only fed us with manna in the wilderness.
Had He only given us the Sabbath to renew our strength.
Had He only brought us to hear him at Mount Sinai
Had He only given us his Torah (the law) to guide us.
Had He only planned to build the Tabernacle his dwelling place.
Had He only brought us to the land He promised to Israel.
Had He only consecrated the Temple He permitted to be build.
Had he only sent Jesus "The Temple not built with hands."

That atonement he made for our sins.

DAYENU - (It is Sufficient)
(1)
ILU HO-TZI HO-TZI A-NU
HO-TZI A-NU MI- MITZ RA-IM,
HO-TZI A-NU MI- MITZ RA-IM DAYENU.
(CHORUS)
DA-DA-YE-NU DA-DA-YE-NU
DA-DA-YE-NU DA-DA-YE-NU DAYENU
(2)
ILU NA-TAN NA-TAN LA-NU
NA-TAN LA-NU ET-HA-TORAH
NA-TAN LA-NU ET-HA-TORAH DAYENU
(CHORUS)
(3)
ILU NA-TAN NA-TAN LA-NU
NA-TAN LA-NU ET-HA-SHABAT
NA-TAN LA-NU ET-HA-SHABAT DAYENU
(CHORUS)
(4)
ILU SHA-LACH SHA-LACH LA-NU
SHA-LACH LA-NU ET-MA-SHI-ACH
SHA-LACH LA-NU ET-MA-SHI-ACH DAYENU
(CHORUS)

- If God just bought us out of Egypt, it would have been sufficient.
- If God just gave us Torah (The Instructions), it would have been sufficient.

- If God just gave us the Sabbath, it would have been sufficient.
- But God also gave us the Messiah (Jesus) IT IS SUFFICIENT!

Blessing over the meal

Traditionally, in a Jewish Seder, a blessing is not made before, but after the meal. Since we are believers in the risen Messiah, we can bless before or after.

The Meal

After the Meal:

The third cup, The **Cup of The Covenant (Redemption)**: This is actually the focal point of the entire ceremony; but the service can't proceed just yet because something is missing. Earlier, something was broken, buried, and now needs to be brought back. What was it?

The Search for the Afikomen

All of the children are supposed to search the home for the Afikomen. Then when it is found, the **Afikomen** will be broken into olive size pieces and distributed to everyone at the table. This matzah eaten after dinner is taken with the third cup. **"The Cup of Redemption"**

This is the origin of our communion service.

Where else can we find a clearer picture or our Messiah Jesus than in this custom concerning the Afikomen, which is broken, buried, and then brought back? The matzah, which is unleavened—a symbol of a sinless nature—speaks of Messiah.

The rabbis have created some very specific rules concerning the appearance of matzah if it is to be used at Passover.

1) It must be striped. ***Jesus was striped.***

As the prophet Isaiah foretold, "And with his stripes we are healed." Isaiah 53:5

2) It must be pierced. ***Jesus was pierced.***

As the prophet Zachariah foretold, "They shall look upon Me whom they have pierced." Zechariah 12:10; John 19:37

3) It must be bruised. ***Jesus was bruised.***

"But he was wounded for our transgressions, he was bruised for our iniquities: the chastisement of our peace was upon him." Isaiah 53:5

We can also see our Messiah not only in the Afikomen, but in the Matzah-tosh as well.

Do you remember the pouch containing the three layers of matzah from which the Afikomen was drawn?

There some disagreement among our rabbis about the meaning of this pouch -- this mysterious three-in-one bag. Some teach that the Matzah-Tosh represents the three patriarchs of Israel: Abraham, Isaac, and Jacob. But this doesn't explain why is the middle matzah broken, burred, and then brought back. Others say that the matzah-tosh represents the divisions of worship in the ancient kingdom: the priests, the Levites, and the people of Israel, but again, why is the middle matzah broken, buried, and then brought back? Still others teach us that the matzah-tosh represents three crowns: the crown of learning, the crown of priesthood, and the crown of kingship, But why is the middle matzah broken, burred, and then brought back?

For the traditional Jewish person, the answer isn't known. And none of these explanations give a satisfactory answer.

But why even search for explanations? Why not just accept the answer that is suggested so clearly in the very design of the Matzah-Tosh itself? There are three layers to the Mazah-Tosh and together they form a triune object. There is a Hebrew word which refers to such a unity. This word is **echad.** And it brings to mind the words of God given to us through Moses who declared,

> **"Shema Yisrael Adonai Eloheynu Adonai Echad." "Hear, O Israel, the lord our God, the Lord is One."** Deuteronomy 6:4

But the word used for one is echad - a unity creating *one* unique thing. At Passover the head of the household removes the middle layer of this unity -- this echad. It is made visible while the other two remain hidden from our view. They are not even eaten at the Seder.

> **"In the beginning was the Word, and the Word was with God and the Word was God." (John 1:1)**
>
> **And the Word became flesh and dwelt among us. (John 1:14)**
>
> **And He came unto his own, but his own received Him not (John 1:11).**
>
> **But as many as received Him to them He gave the right to become the Children of God. Even to those who believe on His name. (John 1:12)"**

Jewish people who know the Messiah know that the unity of the Matzah-Tosh bears witness to the unity of one God revealed in three persons: God the Father, God the Son, and

God the Holy Spirit. Why is the middle matzah broken, buried and then brought back? We know it is because Jesus was broken, buried and then brought back. In 1 Corinthians 11:24 Jesus is recorded taking bread (Matzah), breaking it as He said,

> **"Take, eat: this is my body, which is broken for you: this do in remembrance of me."**

This issue of the **echad** in Deuteronomy 6:4 has been so contentious for the Jewish people throughout history that some Rabbis even advocated changing the scripture to the *other* Hebrew word for "one" that itself leaves no place for the concept of a "unity." Thankfully, the scriptural purists have consistently won the battle!

However, there is still more! Yeshua took on the form of a man when he came to the earth. In doing so he took on the form of the "bread of the earth." When he died and rose from the dead he became the "bread of life.[32]" This Afikomen after dinner then represents Yeshua as the bread of life that was resurrected from the dead!

---

[32] John 6:35

The Third Cup

It is now time for the third cup, the Cup of the Covenant (or Redemption). The fruit of the vine at Passover is always New Wine, and it must be red and sweet. Our rabbis say this is to remind us of the precious blood of the first Passover lamb—the lamb of the covenant. That lamb was sacrificed so that we might be redeemed—brought back—from slavery and bondage to Pharaoh, brought back (in faith) to follow the God of Israel. In the same way, the blood of another Passover lamb, the Messiah Jesus, was sacrificed in order to buy us back, to redeem us from bondage and slavery to sin. It was concerning this third cup, the Cup of Redemption, the cup taken after dinner, that the Messiah Yeshua said, as revealed in 1 Corinthians 11:25,

> **"This cup which is poured out for you is the new covenant in my blood: this do as often as you drink, in remembrance of me."**

This is the new covenant promised to us by God through the prophet Jeremiah when he declared,

> "Behold, days are coming when I will make a new covenant with the house of Israel and the house of Judah. Not like the covenant which I made with their fathers in the day that I took them by the hand to bring them out of the land of Egypt; my covenant which they broke, although I was a husband to

them. But this is the covenant which I will make with the house of Israel. After those days I will put my Law within them, and on their hearts will I write it. And I will be their God and they shall be my people." (Jer. 31:31-33)

The Cup of Redemption and the broken piece of Afikomen are now taken together in remembrance of the blood and the body of the Passover lamb. Let's give thanks for our Passover Lamb, Jesus.

However, we are also supposed to be reminded of the Jewish wedding ceremony in the way in which Jesus took the Cup and dedicated the Bread. He was performing the ritual as a Bridegroom making promises to his future Bride, saying even as the Bridegrooms of his day that he was going to go and prepare a place for her and that he would come and take her back with him to his father's house! (John 14:2-3)

(Eat and Drink)

Cup of Elijah

There is one more cup that we haven't talked about. This a cup from which no one drinks. This is the Cup of Elijah. It is traditional in Jewish homes at Passover that an entire place setting is left untouched for the prophet Elijah. Why is that? The Hebrew Prophet Malachi wrote that before the Messiah comes, he would be preceded by the return of Elijah the Prophet, Elliyahu Hanavi. Because of this prophecy, each year at Passover, a child goes to the door and opens it wide, hoping that the prophet will enter the home and announce the coming of Messiah.

Traditionally the door is opened

Jewish believers know that Eli-ahu, Elijah had returned. For when Jesus spoke of the prophet John, He said of him, **"If you care to**

accept it, he himself is Elijah, who was to come." (Matthew 11:14) The prophet, the forerunner, has come in the person of John the Baptist who announced, "Behold the Lamb of God who takes away the sin of the world." (John 1:29) Our Messiah is Jesus.

There is another song that is sung before the closing of the Passover Seder (by Jewish people around the world), and although it is sung with enthusiasm during the Seder today, many years ago, it was sung with deep remorse and deep longing for the messiah to come through the announcement by Elijah the Prophet.

Eliyahu Ha-Navi

אֵלִיָּהוּ הַנָּבִיא, אֵלִיָּהוּ הַתִּשְׁבִּי, אֵלִיָּהוּ, אֵלִיָּהוּ, אֵלִיָּהוּ הַגִּלְעָדִי,
בִּמְהֵרָה בְיָמֵינוּ יָבֹא אֵלֵינוּ עִם מָשִׁיחַ בֶּן דָּוִד, עִם מָשִׁיחַ בֶּן דָּוִד.

Elijah the prophet, Elijah the Tishbite, Elijah the Gileadite.
May he come quickly, in our days, with the Messiah, the son of David.

It is important to remember that not all Jewish people in this world know Yeshua (Jesus) as Lord and Savior. Therefore as believers we like to take a few minutes to pray for them to know the blessed hope that we know to be true: That Messiah has come and his name is Yeshua (Jesus)!

> ¹¹ "I say then, they did not stumble so as to fall, did they? May it never be! But by their transgression, salvation *has come* to the Gentiles, to make them jealous. ¹² Now if their transgression is riches for the world and their failure is riches for the Gentiles, how much more will their [f]fulfillment be! ¹³ But I am speaking to you who are Gentiles. Inasmuch then as I am an apostle of Gentiles, I magnify my ministry, ¹⁴ if somehow I might move to jealousy my [g]fellow countrymen and save some of them.¹⁵ For if their rejection is the reconciliation of the world, what will *their* acceptance be but life from the dead?" Romans 11:11-15

God still has a purpose and calling for Israel and all believers need to pray for its fulfillment!

> ²⁵ Lest you be wise in your own sight, I want you to understand this mystery, brothers: a partial hardening has come upon Israel, until the fullness of the Gentiles has come in. ²⁶ And in this way all Israel will be saved, as it is written,
>
> "The Deliverer will come from Zion,
>   he will banish ungodliness from Jacob";

²⁷ "and this will be my covenant with them
   when I take away their sins."

²⁸ As regards the gospel, they are enemies of God for your sake. But as regards election, they are beloved for the sake of their forefathers. ²⁹ For the gifts and the calling of God are irrevocable. ³⁰ For just as you were at one time disobedient to God but now have received mercy because of their disobedience, ³¹ so they too have now been disobedient in order that by the mercy shown to you *they also may now receive mercy*. ³² For God has consigned all to disobedience, that he may have mercy on all.

³³ Oh, the depth of the riches and wisdom and knowledge of God! How unsearchable are his judgments and how inscrutable his ways!

³⁴ "For who has known the mind of the Lord,
   or who has been his counselor?"
³⁵ "Or who has given a gift to him
   that he might be repaid?"

³⁶ For from him and through him and to him are all things. To him be glory for ever. Amen.

The Fourth Cup

We now come to the forth cup, the Cup of Hallel or the Cup of Praise.

Yeshua Jesus did not drink of this cup. We read in Luke 22:18 (NIV)

"For I tell you I will not drink again of the fruit of the vine until the kingdom of God comes."

Again, saying precisely the words that a Bridegroom in his days would, he stated he would not drink of the special cup again until his wedding day. For a traditional Jewish bride and bridegroom they waited a mere year, while we've been waiting a much longer time for our Marriage Supper with the Lamb! (Revelation 19: 6-9).

We will drink of the fourth cup either, and rejoice in celebration of His triumphant return. Through Yeshua (Jesus), we have been redeemed from the slavery of sin out of every tongue, tribe, nation and people!

Next Year in Jerusalem!

Every Seder concludes with the hope that next year Messiah will come, and that we will be celebrating the Passover next year in Jerusalem.

For those of us that know the Risen Savior, we have the same hope.  But our hope is לשנה הבאה בירושלים! that next year we will be celebrating it with Yeshua (Jesus' Hebrew Name) when he returns.

This year we celebrate the Passover here,

NEXT YEAR IN JERUSALEM

L'SHA-NA HA-HAH B'RU-SHA-LA-YIM
L'SHA-NA HA-HAH B'RU-SHA-LA-YIM
(Twice)

Passover

318 L'Shana Ha Ba'ah

Next year in Jerusalem!

לְשָׁנָה הַבָּאָה בִּירוּשָׁלַיִם.

Author's Biographies

__Tov Rose__

Tov Rose, founder
The Entertainment Industry Chaplains
PO BOX 22231 | Saint Paul | MN 55122
e-mail: chaplains@thechaplains.org
www.TheChaplains.org | www.TovRose.com
Saint Paul: 651-686-5600
Fax: 845-698-5600

TOV Rose is the Radio Host of To The Jew First Radio, featured on 980AM KKMS.com. He is the author of several books, including *The Book of GOD*, *The New Messianic Version of the Bible*, *The Paranormal GOD*, *The Seams of the Hebrew Bible, The Baptism of Jesus from a Jewish Perspective,* and *The Fall of the American Babylon*--on Amazon.

Tov is a Conference Speaker, producer, performer, Bible teacher, chaplain, pastor and founder of The Entertainment Industry Chaplains. For more than 20 years he has been active working with people to help them better understand God, the Jewishness of Jesus, and live more fulfilling lives.

When not writing books and all those other things, he enjoys quiet times at home with his wife, children and praying together with a group of grandmothers who have the uncanny knack of being able to bend God's ear.

Specializing in teaching the things other people don't, TOV has a reputation for teaching solid Bible foundations and difficult to understand Biblical concepts in a compassionate simple manner that anyone can understand. He is not one to shy away difficult and taboo subjects. He has ministered, performed and taught at literally thousands of congregations, Bible conferences and seminars world-wide, sharing his unique perspectives and passion for people, for God and for Biblical truths.

Victims of Child Sexual Abuse and Christian Organizational Spiritual Abuse, TOV and his wife, Michelle, have been involved with helping protect children online and adult victims recover.

Tov has served on the staff of four Congregations, several Para-church organizations, been a church planter, and currently serves on the Board of Directors for Midwest Hebrew Ministries, on the leadership team of a Messianic Congregational Church Plant in Lakeville, MN, and with Gospel Café Ministries, International.

In addition to practical ministry experience and education, Tov has studied Biblical Hebrew and Theology with Dr. John H. Sailhamer, and Biblical Greek with Dr. David Alan Black. He was also allowed the unique privilege to experience an intensive long-term private tutorship in the subjects of Jewish and Rabbinic Theology, Christian & Messianic Theology, Thought & Literature; Hebrew, Yiddish, Biblical Research, and much more, with Dr. Louis Goldberg (deceased), Professor Emeritus and 30-year Chairman of the Jewish Studies Department at Moody Bible Institute, Chicago.

TOV guests on radio programs, television shows, and speaks at conferences, seminars and in local congregations worldwide.

Find out more at www.tovrose.com

Michelle Rose

Michelle's parents are believers. She was raised knowing she was Jewish and Jesus is Messiah. During college, she sensed a call on her life to share the Messiah with her people. After graduation she moved to New York City to work in Jewish missions. There they met, and were married in 1998. In 2003, they moved to my hometown, Minneapolis, Minnesota, representing Chosen People Ministries and ministering in the South-Metro area.

Our heart's desire is to see all people, Jewish and Gentile, experience the life-changing love of our Heavenly Father through Jesus our Messiah.

Mike Rose

**Michael Rose
Yad Vered HaSharon
Ministries (aka: Rose of
Sharon Ministries of
Minnesota)**

Yad Veredf HaSharon Ministries is a non-denominational ministry which teaches Scripture within its cultural and historical context revealing often misunderstood concepts in the Word.

Michael is a Jewish believer in the Messiah Jesus, born to secular parents. At the age of three his mother passed away, and his father, being too busy to raise three young children, relinquished the responsibility of raising Michael and his two sisters to their grandparents who were Conservative Jews. Michael often spent time with his orthodox great aunt and uncle. While studying for his bar-mitzvah, starting at the age of eleven, reading and studying the Prophets and the Writings, he started asking numerous questions of the Rabbis concerning issues about the promised messiah, sin and salvation. When the Rabbis couldn't satisfy his curiosity, he started searching for answers on his own. After meeting, and marrying his lovely wife, Linda, in 1969, he discovered the New Testament, through friends, and soon realized that the answers to all his unanswered questions were contained within the Bible.

After moving to Minnesota, Michael, Linda, and their three children attended a messianic congregation where they realized that there was a need for Christian churches to understand the historical and cultural roots of their faith, and for Jews to understand that Jesus is the promised Messiah that they have been waiting for for over twenty-five hundred years; so in 1996 they started Rose of Sharon Ministries of Minnesota, but in 2009 decided to use the Hebrew translation Yad Vered HaSharon Ministries. Michael, a teacher by trade, started working toward his Masters of Divinity at Bethel Seminary in 2001, where he enjoyed debating his professors, but had to withdraw, for financial reasons in 2004, when his teaching position of eleven years was eliminated. After retiring, Michael decided to finish his Master's Degree, and is currently studying for his MA in Biblical and Theological Studies, at Knox Theological Seminary. Michael has taught in many churches in the Upper Mid-West, and has had conducted a bi-weekly Bible study, in his home, for the past ten years. Michael's three children are all in ministry.

Michael has written numerous pamphlets and teachings. He serves on the Board of Directors for Midwest Hebrew Ministries. He is the CFO of The Gospel Café Ministries, a 501(c)3 corporation which will be opening up high quality Coffee and Outreach Centers on and near college and university campuses in the United States. He is a commentator on a weekly radio show "To The Jew First" on KKMS 980 AM Radio, in the Twin Cities. He has been a guest on other local radio shows. He has been working with his younger son, for the past several years, raising support for Tikvat Yisrael Messianic School, a private elementary school, which will be opening its doors for students in the Fall of 2015 in Tel Aviv, Israel. And often speaks and teaches in churches around the Mid-West as part of the MHM Speakers Bureau.

Made in the USA
Charleston, SC
09 August 2014